THE LORD'S MY SHEPHERD, I'LL NOT WANT ...

THE LORD'S MY SHEPHERD, I'LL NOT WANT ...

Some Fresh Insights into Your Favourite Psalm

by

Timothy J. E. Cross
B.A., B.D., P.G.C.E., Th.D

AMBASSADOR

Belfast Northern Ireland Greenville South Carolina

The Lord's My Shepherd, I'll Not Want
© Copyright 2000 Timothy Cross

ISBN 1 84030 074 4

Ambassador Publications
a division of
Ambassador Productions Ltd.
Providence House
Ardenlee Street,
Belfast,
BT6 8QJ
Northern Ireland
www.ambassador-productions.com

Emerald House
427 Wade Hampton Blvd.
Greenville
SC 29609, USA
www.emeraldhouse.com

DEDICATION

To my little nieces, Alice and Rebecca, with the prayer that in due time they will come to know and love the Shepherd of this Psalm.

CONTENTS

AUTHOR'S PREFACE

"**THE LORD'S MY SHEPHERD**, I'll not want . . . " Psalm 23 is probably the favourite Psalm of most people, and a strong candidate for the most well known and recited passage in all the Scriptures. Here we are dealing with some of the most beautiful and breath-taking poetry ever penned - a most precious gift of the Lord to the individual believer personally and the universal Church collectively.

In Psalm 23 the Holy Spirit has not only bequeathed to us the most exquisite verse however, but also some of the most lofty theology and some of the most comforting truth. It is this which makes Psalm 23 the 'Psalm for all occasions' that it is:-

When sung at a wedding, Psalm 23 enhances the occasion's joy. When sung at a funeral, Psalm 23 is an incalculable source of divine comfort. When read by the bed of sickness or during the dark night of the soul, when all human comfort has gone, this Psalm never fails to bring spiritual healing in its wake. When we get alone with our Saviour and read this Psalm, we are assured that, the dangers, difficulties, doubts and disappointments in our lives apart, all is well with our souls.

In the following pages we will seek to cast fresh light on this ancient Psalm. Whilst the Psalm is well-known, one wonders just how many of the Lord's people really understand its true meaning. We will therefore consider the Psalm in the light of the whole Bible and also, most importantly, in the context of its original, pastoral setting in the Middle East. Our familiarity with the Psalm must not blunt its full force or deny us the fullness of the blessing which it was designed by God to give.

The blessing I received during the preparation of this work was immense. My hope and prayer is that yours will be the same now as you read on. May the Lord be pleased to take up and use what follows to give you increased understanding in your mind, greater joy in your heart and more love in your soul for the Good Shepherd Who laid down His life for the sheep.

Timothy J. E. Cross
Barry, S. Wales

A PSALM OF DAVID

The LORD is my shepherd, I shall not want;
He makes me lie down in green pastures.
He leads me beside still waters;
He restores my soul.
He leads me in paths of righteousness for His name's sake.

Even though I walk through the valley of the shadow of death,
I fear no evil,
For Thou art with me;
Thy rod and Thy staff,
they comfort me.

Thou preparest a table before me
in the presence of my enemies;
Thou anointest my head with oil;
my cup overflows.
Surely goodness and mercy shall follow me
all the days of my life;
and I shall dwell in the house of the LORD for ever.

(Psalm 23)

Chapter One

THE DIVINE PASTOR

The LORD is my shepherd, I shall not want (v.1)

THE OPENING VERSE OF Psalm 23 actually contains the whole of the Psalm in embryo. The first verse is the 'seed-plot' of the whole Psalm, for the remaining lines are simply an unfolding, explaining and expanding of this one over-all theme of the tender care which Almighty God has for His sheep, in both time and eternity. If the Lord really is my shepherd, then certain consequences and implications are sure to follow.

David himself, the human author of this Psalm, was originally a shepherd before he went on to higher things. It was said of him *behold, he is keeping the sheep* (1 Samuel 16:11). In the providence of God, this early experience of his was to be used as a formative training for the time when he would exchange his role from being a shepherd of sheep to that of being king - leading the flock of the nation of Israel. *He chose David His servant, and took him from the sheepfolds; from tending the ewes that had young he brought him to be the shepherd of Jacob His people, of Israel His inheritance. With upright heart he tended them, and guided them with skilful hand* (Psalm 78:70-72).

David was thus well schooled in matters pastoral, and the Holy Spirit employed this early education and expertise he had gained to reveal to him the most amazing, awesome and comforting spiritual truth: that the relationship between God and His people may be likened to that of the relationship between a shepherd and his sheep. The theme may be traced elsewhere in the Scriptures:-

For He is our God, and we are the people of His pasture, and the sheep of His hand (Psalm 95:7)

He will feed His flock like a shepherd, He will gather the lambs in His arms, He will carry them in His bosom, and gently lead those that are with young (Isaiah 40:11)

The image then is taken from a familiar earthly scene which David knew well. Yet the spiritual reality behind the image will transcend time on earth and continue on for all eternity in heaven, for Revelation 7:17 says of the redeemed in glory that *the Lamb in the midst of the throne will be their shepherd, and He will guide them to springs of living water; and God will wipe away every tear from their eyes.*

The LORD is my shepherd . . . The opening verse of Psalm 23 introduces us to the Divine Pastor. A Pastor Who is a peerless, present and a personal Pastor.

1. A Peerless Pastor

The LORD is my shepherd. Who is the Lord? He is the God of creation and the God of the covenant. He is the maker and sustainer of all things. He is 'infinite, eternal and unchangeable in His being, wisdom, power, holiness, justice, goodness and truth.' He is the God of amazing grace Who in

Christ actually became a man and walked this earth, and lived and died and rose again 'for us men and for our salvation.' The Divine Pastor of Psalm 23 is One Who saves, keeps and satisfies His people and brings them surely and safely to bask in the glory of His house for ever. The Lord is a peerless Pastor - peerless in His Person and peerless in His love for His own. His pastoral care is without compare.

2. A Present Pastor

The LORD is my shepherd. The God of the Bible is ever present and always available for His people. The Shepherd-King of the Bible cannot be contained or hindered by time and space. He is the God *Who is and Who was and Who is to come* (Revelation 1:4). He is the God Who is behind us, with us and before us. That the Lord *is* my present shepherd and pastor is a source of great comfort and strength to the individual believer - especially amidst the present distresses and difficulties of the current hour. *God is our refuge and strength, a very present help in trouble* (Psalm 46:1).

> *Yesterday God helped me*
> *Today He'll do the same*
> *How long will this continue?*
> *For ever, praise His Name!*

3. A Personal Pastor

The LORD is my shepherd. Martin Luther used to say that true religion is a matter of personal pronouns. *My beloved is mine and I am his . . .* (Song of Solomon 2:16). The greatest wonder of all is the message that sinners like ourselves may yet enjoy a personal relationship and friendship with none less than God Himself. *He calls His own sheep by name* (John 10:3).

The Faith of the Bible proclaims that sinful creatures may know the holy Creator as a child knows its father, a subject knows a king or as a sheep knows its shepherd. How is it possible when the gulf between a holy God and a sinful humanity is so infinite? The answer of the Bible is 'through Jesus Christ our Lord.' *For there is one God and there is one mediator between God and men, the Man Christ Jesus* (1 Timothy 2:5). Through personal faith in the crucified Saviour, our sins are forgiven and we are reconciled to God and so may enjoy God's friendship, favour and fellowship for both time and eternity. *The LORD is my shepherd. The Lord knows those who are His* (2 Timothy 2:19). Jesus said *I am the Good Shepherd; I know My own and My own know Me* (John 10:14). When we are objects of His care it is as though we are the only concern He has in all the universe!

Our Shepherd Care

The LORD is my shepherd . . . The verse sums up so much. It tells of the close, personal relationship between God and His own. It speaks of His vigilant care and it speaks of our Shepherd's authority and love. It speaks of the constant company and companionship enjoyed by God and His people. It assures us that almighty God Himself has undertaken to feed us, guide us, protect us and care and provide for us in every conceivable way. Our earthly and eternal well-being is God's concern! *The LORD is my shepherd.* It is both a personal testimony and a statement of Faith.

Our Shepherd Christ

i. The Person of the Shepherd

In John 10:11 the Lord Jesus Christ made the most staggering and startling claim. He says there *I am the Good*

Shepherd. The claim is startling, as it is a claim to deity - if it were not true it would be totally blasphemous. The statement reveals that the Shepherd of the Old Testament and the Shepherd of the New Testament have equal parity, for the God of the Old Testament refers to Himself as the great I AM - *I AM WHO I AM* (Exodus 3:14) just as He is also referred to as the Good Shepherd (Psalm 23, Ezekiel 34 et al). Jesus's claim to be the Good Shepherd then was actually a claim to be God, and would have been perceived to be so by His followers, well versed in Scripture as they were. The claim though is in-line with everything else recorded in the Bible about the life and ministry of the Lord Jesus: Here we are dealing with God in the flesh. It is one of the fundamental fundamentals of the Christian Faith. Christianity is Christ and Jesus Christ is God! *He who has seen Me has seen the Father* (John 14:9). *He who does not honour the Son does not honour the Father Who sent Him* (John 5:23).

ii. The Passion of the Shepherd

As the Good Shepherd, Christ cares intimately, eternally and sacrificially for His sheep. In full, John 10:11 reads *I am the Good Shepherd, the Good Shepherd lays down His life for the sheep.* And the Lord Jesus did indeed lay down His life for His sheep, when He died on Calvary's cross as our sacrifice and substitute. Peter explained *Christ also died for sins once for all, the righteous for the unrighteous, that He might bring us to God* (1 Peter 3:18).

iii. The People of the Shepherd

Confessing *The LORD is my shepherd* then amounts to the same thing as knowing the Lord Jesus Christ as our own personal Saviour and Friend. He gave His life for the sheep in the past, and He currently shares His life with His sheep in

the present and will provide for His sheep in the future. Small
wonder then that David went on to testify *I shall not want* -
and all Christ's people may say the same. The force of the
verb could be paraphrased as: 'I have not wanted, I do not
want and I do not expect ever to want, because the Lord is my
shepherd.' Although David was in the barren wilderness - a
place of want - he did not want, for he knew the Lord. In the
place of nothing he lacked nothing, as God was his God. It
has been well said that 'When God is all you have, you will
find that He is all you need.' *My God will supply every need of
yours according to His riches in glory in Christ Jesus* (Philippians
4:19).

And so the opening verse sets both the scene and the
theme for the rest of this Psalm of Psalms. We have a Divine
Pastor! *The LORD is my shepherd.* The details and implications of this wonderful fact are now expounded and explained
in the verses that follow.

> *The King of love my shepherd is*
> *Whose goodness faileth never*
> *I nothing lack if I am His*
> *And He is mine for ever.*

Chapter Two

THE DIVINE PASTURES

He makes me lie down in green pastures . . . (v.2).

ONE OF THE PRIMARY tasks of a Pastor is to feed the flock of God and to attend generally to their overall spiritual well being. The risen Christ's command to Peter was *Feed My lambs . . . Tend My sheep . . . Feed My sheep . . .* (John 21:15-17). Peter himself was to become an undershepherd in the church - a shepherd under the Chief Shepherd - and he in turn encouraged his fellow pastors to *Tend the flock of God that is your charge* (1 Peter 5:2). A shepherd of souls feeds his flock with a steady diet of the Word of God. A shepherd of sheep however feeds his flock by leading them to green pastures. In the green pastures the flock can lie down in safety and graze leisurely on the nourishing grass.

David's early years as a shepherd would have seen him pastoring a flock in the Judean wilderness. The Judean wilderness is a very barren place - a desert. In such a place, green pasture suitable for sheep is somewhat rare. As a good shepherd his knowledge of geography would equal his knowledge of his flock. A good shepherd would know the lie of the land. He would know the whereabouts of the scrub land, and so be able to lead his flock to this nourishing pasture-land so vital to a sheep's physical health and well being. With these thoughts in mind, David lifted his eyes heavenward and thought of God Himself. *The LORD is my shepherd . . . He makes me lie down in green pastures.* The verse informs us of both a needed rest and a nourishing sustenance.

i. A Needed Rest

He makes me lie down in green pastures . . . Such a lying down would be most welcome to a weary sheep, having followed the shepherd through the wilderness for miles, wandering from one pasture land to another.

Salvation, in the Bible, is depicted in many ways, but perhaps the easiest to understand is that of 'rest.' Jesus once gave a lovely invitation to those struggling along wearily, aware of their load of sin. He said and still says *Come to Me, all who labour and are heavy laden, and I will give you rest. Take My yoke upon you, and learn from Me; for I am gentle and lowly in heart, and you will find rest for your souls* (Matthew 11:28).

I heard the voice of Jesus say
'Come unto Me and rest
Lay down, thou weary one, lay down
Thy head upon My breast!'
I came to Jesus as I was
Weary and worn and sad
I found in Him a resting place
And He has made me glad.

We who have believed enter that rest . . . (Hebrews 4:3).

Lying down in the pleasant green pastures also tells of the blessed peace which results from the rest of God's salvation. The believing soul enjoys peace with God as a consequence of Christ's saving death on the cross. Colossians 1:20 tells of His *making peace by the blood of His cross.* Romans 5:1 declares *Therefore, since we are justified by faith, we have peace with God through our Lord Jesus Christ.* It is by the death of Jesus that our sins are forgiven and we have peace with God. God's sheep then enjoy the divinely bestowed rest of God's salvation.

ii. A Nourishing Sustenance

He makes me lie down in green pastures . . . The God Who saves us by His grace also leads us and feeds us by the same grace. Our souls are saved by the Word of God and they are also sustained by the Word of God. *Man shall not live by bread alone, but by every word that proceeds from the mouth of God* (Matthew 4:4). It is the Word of God - both read in private and expounded in public - which provides us with the needed spiritual nourishment for our souls and makes us grow spiritually strong. . . . *the Word of His grace . . . is able to build you up* (Acts 20:32). *Nourished on the words of the faith and of the good doctrine which you have followed* (1 Timothy 4:6). We thus neglect the Bible at our peril. C. H. Spurgeon wrote the following:-

> What are these *green pastures* but the Scriptures of truth - always fresh, always rich, and never exhausted? There is no fear of biting the bare ground where the grass is long enough for the flock to lie down in it. Sweet and full are the doctrines of the gospel. Fit food for souls, as tender grass is natural nutriment for sheep. When by faith we are

enabled to find rest in the promises, we are like the
sheep that lie down in the midst of the pasture. We
find at the same moment provender and peace, rest
and refreshment, serenity and satisfaction.

Bearing the above in mind, take a 'spiritual medical'.
How is your appetite for the Word of God? Do you *Like
new-born babes, long for the pure spiritual milk; that by it you may
grow up to salvation; for you have tasted the kindness of the Lord*
(1 Peter 2:2,3).When all is spiritually well with us, we will
hunger for the Word of God.

A sound nutrition is as essential for our spiritual life as
it is for our physical life, so we need the whole Word of God -
solid food - and not just those parts of it which we find
especially sweet and agreeable. The Bible provides us with a
variety of nourishing food for our souls - food which
energises our spiritual life:- *Thy words were found and I did eat
them, and Thy words became to me a joy and the delight of my heart*
(Jeremiah 15:16). *How sweet are Thy words to my taste, sweeter
than honey to my mouth* (Psalm 119:103).

The Lord our shepherd then, through Christ the Good
Shepherd, bestows on us the blessed rest of salvation, and
sustains us by providing us with necessary and agreeable
spiritual food on our journey to glory. *The LORD is my
shepherd, I shall not want.* Without rest we wear out. Without
food we starve. In Christ, God graciously provides His
people with both. If we belong to Jesus we will never be
lacking in anything that is essential for our true well being.

*I never shall want, for the Lord is my shepherd
And who ever lacked that was under His care?
He makes me lie down in the fairest of pastures
Where soft flow the waters, He leadeth me there.*

We shall consider these 'soft waters' in the next chapter.

Chapter Three

THE DIVINE PROVISION

He leads me beside still waters . . . (v.2).

Water for the Body

AS FOOD AND WATER are high on the list of a sheep's essential requirements, a good shepherd will ensure that they are suitably provided with both. Food has already been considered in relation to the *green pastures* - and will be considered again in the verse *Thou preparest a table for me . . .* (v. 5). But we come now to the basic physical need for water. Water is essential for life. Whilst we can last for up to forty days without food, we cannot last for more than a few days without water.

In contrast to our temperate climate here in the West, where it seems to rain a lot, water is at a premium in Israel, where the climate is such that after the rainy season it does not rain for months on end. The good shepherd then, knowing the lie of the land along with the need of his flock, will lead his sheep to the water supply so that they can drink and stay well. *He leads me beside still waters . . .* A little background information will aid our understanding of this term *still waters* :-

The Eastern Background

Sheep are unable to drink from fast flowing water, even if they are extremely thirsty. The anatomy of the sheep is such that its nose and mouth are very close together. Drinking from a fast stream of rushing water would therefore be uncomfortable for it. The water would go up its nose, and the discomfort would cause it to cough and splutter and turn away from the water it needs. A good shepherd therefore ensures that his flock is led to *still waters* - drinkable water suitable for the requirements and need of his flock.

In Israel, fast flowing torrents of water may be seen from time to time, most notably in the rainy season, after a downpour. At such a time, the dry river beds - known as wadis - become powerful torrents of water. A tender lamb would be frightened by its roar and would not even approach it. Thirsty though it might be, with a plentiful supply of water at hand, it would yet be unwilling to drink from such a roaring stream. A good shepherd would therefore take his staff and dig a small pit by the stream. Into this the fast flowing waters would flow, be contained and become still. This pool of still water would then meet the requirements of the sheep exactly. *He leads me beside still waters* - whereupon the thirsty sheep could drink freely, having its thirst quenched and its physical health restored.

Water for the Soul

As there can be no physical life without a supply of clean, suitable water, similarly, there can be no spiritual life without adequate water too. The Bible enunciates a water for the soul - a life-giving water which brings eternal salvation, eternal satisfaction and eternal satiation when we are led to it and drink from it. The Bible uses the metaphor of having our thirst quenched - one to which we can all relate on a hot summer's day - to describe what it is to be saved:-

With joy you will draw water from the wells of salvation (Isaiah 12:3).

Revelation 7:16 ff. describes salvation in terms of eternal satisfaction - an eternal satisfaction with God's all-sufficient and super-abundant provision for our need in Jesus Christ. We read of the redeemed in glory here: *They shall hunger no more, neither thirst any more* . . . *For the Lamb in the midst of the throne will be their shepherd, and He will guide them to springs of living water.*

The Good Shepherd's Glorious Springs

Jesus, our Good Shepherd, ensures that His sheep are well provided for with life-giving water. He Himself undertakes here for our need. John 7:37 tells us of a public invitation which Jesus once gave - an invitation which still holds today. Jesus said *If anyone thirst, let him come to Me and drink. He who believes in Me, as the Scripture has said, 'Out of his heart shall flow rivers of living water.'* John 4 describes a similar invitation which Jesus once gave in private to a somewhat disreputable woman as they both sat down beside a well. Pointing to the well, Jesus said to her *Every one who drinks of this water will thirst again, but whoever drinks of the water that I shall give him will never thirst; the water that I shall give him will become in him a spring of water, welling up to eternal life* (John 4:13,14). The message here is that only Jesus can satisfy the parched soul. The message here is that the water of this world will finally fail, and leave us eternally thirsty and dissatisfied if we pursue these waters to the detriment of a saving relationship with the Lord Jesus Christ. How many have pursued the waters of this world - career, money, success, status, possessions, illicit thrills - only to find them failing when it really counts? The hymn writer said it well:-

> *I tried the broken cisterns, Lord*
> *But ah! the waters failed*
> *Ee'n as I stooped to drink, they fled*
> *And mocked me as I wailed.*

The Drought of Hell and the Draught of Heaven

This world, apart from Christ, will leave us thirsty and parched for the life-giving water which Christ alone can give. To die without Christ is the worst scenario of all, for a Christless death will see our souls in an eternal hell of thirst, never to be quenched. Hell is a thirsty place. Jesus Himself once described one of the damned there, crying out for relief:- *and in Hades, being in torment . . . he called out 'Father Abraham, have mercy upon me, and send Lazarus to dip the end of his finger in water and cool my tongue; for I am in anguish in this flame'* (Luke 16:23 ff.).

The Christian however need never fear the condemning thirst of hell. *There is therefore now no condemnation for those who are in Christ Jesus* (Romans 8:1). God's sheep will never perish for lack of water. Hell is certainly a thirsty place of condemnation, but on the cross, when Christ bore our sins and God's just punishment upon them, He delivered us from the dreadful, eternal place of thirst. Paradoxically, on the cross, Christ, the giver of living water, suffered the thirst of hell, so that our thirsty souls could be quenched, and we, the thirsty ones, may enjoy the satisfaction of dwelling eternally alongside the springs of water in heaven. On the cross, some of Christ's final words were these: *I thirst* (John 19:28). John then records how Jesus uttered the triumphant acclamation *It is finished* (John 19:30). For on the cross Christ procured our salvation. Because of His saving work at Calvary, all who trust in Him will never thirst in hell. Jesus bestows eternal salvation. Jesus bestows the living, life-giving water which saves and satisfies for all eternity. He is the Good Shepherd, and as such, all his sheep can testify *He leads me beside still waters* - for we have drunk from these still waters, and in drinking we have slaked our spiritual thirst:-

> *I heard the voice of Jesus say*
> *'Behold I freely give*
> *The living water - thirsty one*
> *Stoop down and drink and live!'*
> *I came to Jesus and I drank*
> *Of that life-giving stream:*
> *My thirst was quenched, my soul revived*
> *And now I live in Him.*

Chapter Four

THE DIVINE PEACE

He restores my soul . . . (v. 3)

BEFORE WE CONSIDER THIS delightful verse in detail, we should note its connection with the previous verse: In being led to the still waters, and in drinking a cool, refreshing draught from them, the soul of the flagging sheep would be restored. The sheep could then give a thankful testimony, and say that in his tender care, my loving shepherd *restores my soul.*

The Hebrew mind had less of a distinction between body and soul - the physical and the spiritual - than perhaps we do today. The Hebrew mind was more holistic. In line with modern psychosomatic medicine, they were aware how the body could affect the soul and the soul could affect the body. An illustration of this may be seen in 1 Samuel 30:11 ff., during the days when David was being hunted, hounded and harassed by Saul. We see here the intimate connection between the body and the soul:-

They found an Egyptian in the open country, and brought him to David; and they gave him bread and he ate, they gave him water to drink, and they gave him a piece of a cake of figs and two clusters of raisins. And when he had eaten, his spirit revived; for he had not eaten bread or drunk water for three days and three nights. Similarly, in Judges 15:19 we read that *when he drank, his spirit returned, and he revived.* We could thus paraphrase our verse as 'He restores my life' or even 'He restores *me*.' We may apply this in two ways:-

1. An Eternal Application

He restores my soul . . . The verb 'restore' may be translated as 'He causes to return' or 'He turns back.' It speaks to us of the eternal salvation which our Good Shepherd has undertaken to procure for His wayward sheep, for salvation involves being restored and reconciled to God.

By nature, we are all far from the Shepherd, and ostracised and alienated from the flock of God. *All we like sheep have gone astray; we have turned every one to his own way* (Isaiah 53:6), but in unfathomable mercy, Christ the Good Shepherd has intervened. In amazing grace He has rounded up His stray sheep, and brought us effectually and eternally back to Himself and into the safety of the fold of the flock of God. Jesus said of Himself: *The Son of Man came to seek and to save the lost* (Luke 19:10).

Jesus once depicted our salvation most graphically using 'stray sheep, seeking shepherd' terms in His famous 'Parable of the Lost Sheep.' The parable teaches us much. It teaches us about our straying folly, but also it teaches us about the infinite value of one human soul. The parable also tells of the infinite grace of the tender shepherd, along with the personal and corporate joy which ensues when one soul is saved. The parable, as it came from the lips of the blessed Shepherd-Saviour Himself, goes as follows:-

What man of you, having a hundred sheep, if he has lost one of them, does not leave the ninety-nine in the wilderness, and go after the one which is lost, until he finds it? And when he has found it, he lays it on his shoulders, rejoicing. And when he comes home, he calls together his friends and his neighbours, saying to them, 'Rejoice with me, for I have found my sheep which was lost.' Just so, I tell you, there will be more joy in heaven over one sinner who repents than over ninety-nine righteous persons who need no repentance (Luke 15:4-7).

The parable obviously made a great impact on Peter. Years later, when he himself was an under-shepherd, he wrote reminding the flock under his care: *you were straying like sheep, but have now returned to the Shepherd and Guardian of your souls* (1 Peter 2:25). *He restores my soul.* Christ is a Shepherd characterised by both seeking and saving grace:-

> *In tenderness He sought me*
> *Weary and sick with sin*
> *And on His shoulders brought me*
> *Back to His fold again . . .*
>
> *O the love that sought me*
> *O the blood that bought me*
> *O the grace that brought me to the fold*
> *Wondrous grace that brought me to the fold!*

2. An Earthly Application

He restores my soul . . . In Psalm 94:19 the Psalmist testified similarly: *When the cares of my heart are many, Thy consolations cheer my soul.* The cares of this life can certainly be many and heavy. Christians are not exempt from trials and tribulations, stresses and strains, losses and crosses, pain and perplexity. All can affect our soul. *Through many tribulations we must enter the kingdom of God* (Acts 14:22). Whilst Christians cannot claim immunity from trouble and distress in this world, we yet have a resource of which the non-Christian knows nothing. We have a Good Shepherd to Whom we can turn: *The LORD is my shepherd, I shall not want.* Many are the times when we can testify that whilst our circumstances seemed unbearably difficult and distressing, and we feared that we were veering off course, God yet restored our souls in His all sufficient grace.

David's Distress and David's Deliverance

David, the human author of our Psalm, was just like us. He too had more than his fair share of the harsh realities of this life. 1 Samuel 30:6 describes a time when *David was greatly distressed.* He had every reason to be so. His current residence had been burned down by an enemy invasion, and his family had been taken captive. All his earthly props had been taken from him, leaving him down and distraught. Worse still, even his own people had turned against him: *the people spoke of stoning him, because all the people were bitter in soul.* Yet the Bible records how *David strengthened himself in the LORD his God* (1 Samuel 30:6).

In our times of distress and difficulty, we too are privileged to do the same as David. We too may wait upon the Lord, and know Him gently but surely restoring our spiritual well-being. *He restores my soul.* Isaiah 40:31 tells us: *They who wait for the LORD shall renew their strength, they shall mount up with wings like eagles, they shall run and not be weary, they shall walk and not faint.*

Strengthening ourselves in the Lord involves turning to Him in the time of our trouble. Strengthening ourselves in the Lord involves meditating on His divine attributes - He is the sovereign God, and all the details of our lives are under His control. Strengthening ourselves in the Lord involves reminding ourselves that our loving Shepherd is 'infinite, eternal and unchangeable in His being, wisdom, power, holiness, justice, goodness and truth.' He is too wise to make mistakes, too kind to be cruel and too powerful to be thwarted in His overall purpose for the blessing of His people and the glory of His name. When we look away from our current plight and look to our Father in heaven, we find that *He restores my soul.* Isaiah 30:15 reads *In returning and rest you shall be saved; in quietness and in trust shall be your strength.* It is just unthinkable that the same God who has eternally restored us to Himself in Christ will not also give us sufficient earthly grace to bear whatever His wisdom sees fit to send our way, as we journey onward to our heavenly home.

The LORD is my shepherd. I shall not want . . . He restores my soul . . .

He restoreth my soul when I'm weary
He giveth me strength day by day
He leads me beside the still waters
He guards me each step of the way.

Chapter Five

THE DIVINE PATHWAYS

He leads me in paths of righteousness for His
name's sake (v. 3).

WE HAVE ALREADY SEEN that one of the primary tasks of
the shepherd is to *feed* his flock. To do this, however, the
shepherd will have to *lead* his flock. He will have to lead them
safely to the green pastures and still waters where they can
graze in peace. Leading and feeding then - guiding and
providing - are inextricably bound together in the work of a
shepherd. A good shepherd will always lead his flock in the
right paths. The well-being of the flock depends upon his
leading them aright - as also does the reputation of the
shepherd himself. Leading the sheep the wrong way would
put a black mark against the shepherd's name and cast doubt
on his ability and character. *He leads me in paths of righteous-*
ness for His name's sake. It is an awesome thought and yet

true, that the Almighty has bound up His good name with the guidance of His sheep.

The Eastern Background

He leads me in paths of righteousness . . . Here in the West, a shepherd tends to drive his sheep from behind. In the East however, the shepherd leads his sheep from the front: When the shepherd moves, the sheep will follow, trusting him implicitly. He knows the way ahead and he will surely lead them in the right paths. The Lord Jesus had this common Palestinian scene in mind when He explained of the shepherd *the sheep hear his voice, and he calls his own sheep by name and leads them out. When he has brought out all his own, he goes before them, and the sheep follow him, for they know his voice* (John 10:3,4).

Thou Our Guide.

That Almighty God still leads His people today is plain from Scripture. In Psalm 32:8 God promises *I will instruct you and teach you the way you should go; I will counsel you with My eye upon you.* Then in Psalm 73:24 the Psalmist says to God *Thou dost guide me with Thy counsel, and afterward Thou wilt receive me to glory.* The latter verse has an interesting parallel in our Psalm. i. *Thou dost guide me with Thy counsel: He leads me in paths of righteousness* ii. *afterward Thou wilt receive me to glory: I shall dwell in the house of the LORD for ever* (v. 6).

Divine guidance is a difficult area for some. A good prayer is *Teach me Thy way, O LORD; and lead me on a level path because of my enemies* (Psalm 27:11). The question is 'How does God guide us today?' He does so in two ways, i. By His Word, and ii. By His Providence, that is by His revealed will and by His secret will.

i. The Revealed Will of God

If we are in need of guidance, our first resort should be the written Word of God, the Bible. *Thy Word is a lamp to my feet and a light to my path* (Psalm 119:105). In the Bible we find the revealed will of God, for in the Bible, God has revealed to us His mind concerning our creation and fall and His way of salvation. In the Bible then we have God's revelation of all we need to know concerning what we are to believe and how we are to behave. We thus ignore the Bible at our peril, for in the Bible we find the will of God. Q. 3 of the *Shorter Catechism* puts it in a nutshell. 'What do the Scriptures principally teach?', it asks. The answer given is this: 'The Scriptures principally teach what man is to believe concerning God, and what duty God requires of man.' Divine guidance then - knowing God's will - can never be divorced from the Word of God or contrary to what is written therein.

> *Lord Thy Word abideth*
> *And our footsteps guideth*
> *Who its truth believeth*
> *Light and joy receiveth.*

ii. The Secret Will of God

He leads the humble in what is right, and teaches the humble His way (Psalm 25:9). Humility is an essential requirement of guidance - the humility to admit that we are ignorant of the future and that God alone is all wise and in sovereign control of every detail of our lives. He alone knows the end from the beginning and will surely bring His purpose to pass.

We have seen that we discover the revealed will of God by carefully and prayerfully reading the Bible. We discover the concealed, secret will of God though only in small steps at a time, day by day, through His providential dealings with us through both the pleasant and painful circumstances He sends our way. Our circumstances are not accidental but providential. Ultimately they are ordered by God Himself, for He has 'foreordained whatsoever comes to pass.'

The sheep is a docile animal, characterised by ignorance. The shepherd alone knows the right way. The 'responsibility' of the sheep then is to trust in his wisdom, submit to his will and humbly follow on, knowing that he has the best interests of his flock at heart. The same may be applied to us as regards our relationship with our Good Shepherd in heaven. Proverbs 3:5,6 exhorts *Trust in the LORD with all your heart and do not rely on your own insight. In all your ways acknowledge Him, and He will make straight your paths.*

That Almighty God is controlling the universe generally and working out His purpose in our lives particularly is plain from Scripture:-

The LORD has established His throne in the heavens, and His kingdom rules over all (Psalm 103:19).

(He) accomplishes all things according to the counsel of His will (Ephesians 1:11).

Then in Matthew 10:29,30 the Lord Jesus Himself assures and re-assures His followers that - chaotic appearances to the contrary - our lives are safely, surely and securely under the firm control of our loving heavenly Father. Jesus said *Are not two sparrows sold for a penny? and not one of them will fall to the ground without your Father's will.* It has been well said that those who see the hand of God in everything can gladly leave everything in the hand of God. God's all wise and all loving and all powerful providence is a source of inestimable comfort to His children. *We know that in everything God works for good with those who love Him, who are called according to His purpose* (Romans 8:28).

Our Guidance: His Glory

In closing, notice that God is as equally concerned to give guidance as we are to receive it. Staggeringly, our verse teaches that God's guidance affects His own reputation as well as our well-being. His divine honour is linked to our human blessing! *He leads me in paths of righteousness <u>for His name's sake.</u>* God's name refers to His revealed character. Names to us are something of a convenient 'tag'. In Bible times however, a person's name was bound up with that person's nature. Amazingly then, our verse reveals that Almighty God has staked His reputation on us. We are saved by grace for His own glory. We tend to think of salvation in terms of personal blessing - and salvation most certainly does bring infinite, immense and eternal personal blessing. Yet salvation, according to the Bible, has an even higher purpose, namely the eternal honour and glory of God - *the praise of His glory* (Ephesians 1:12,14). All this being so, it is just unthinkable to even suggest that the God Who has saved us will not also continue to lead and guide us through this earthly wilderness and eventually lead us safely home. His reputation depends on it, so *He leads me in paths of righteousness for His name's sake.*

Guidance does have its mysteries, but surely the secret is to stay close to the guide - the Good Shepherd Who does all things well. *This is God, our God for ever. He will be our guide for ever* (Psalm 48:14).

All the way my Saviour leads me
What have I to ask beside?
Can I doubt His tender mercy
Who through life has been my guide?
Heavenly peace, divinest comfort
Here by faith in Him to dwell!
For I know whate'er befall me
Jesus doeth all things well.

Chapter Six

THE DIVINE PRESENCE

Even though I walk through the valley of the shadow of death,
I fear no evil; for Thou art with me . . . (v. 4).

THIS VERSE ASSURES US of God's presence with us even
in and amidst the darkest, direst and most dangerous of
circumstances. Amidst the most terrifying of circumstances
there is yet the reality of God. *Thou art with me.*

The change from speaking about God indirectly in the
third person singular - *He makes me . . . He leads me . . . He*
restores my soul . . . He leads me - to addressing Him directly in
the second person singular - *Thou art with me* - is especially
noteworthy. In times of difficulty there is a vast difference
between knowing about the Shepherd - *He* - and actually
knowing the Shepherd personally - *Thou.* Knowing God
personally and so being able to address God personally in
prayer is one of the distinguishing marks of the Faith of the
Bible.

The valley of the shadow of death is sometimes interpreted as referring to the believer's transition from this world to the next. Whilst this is a valid application of the verse - for Christ is a Friend in life, death and for all eternity - the primary sense of the verse is very much rooted on earth in this world. Remember that the original setting of Psalm 23 is in the land of Israel, amongst the Judean hills.

The Eastern Background

Picture again the eastern shepherd. He is leading his flock from green pasture to green pasture. Here is our God. He leads His flock from blessing to blessing. In leading the flock to the green pastures however, both shepherds may see fit to lead their flock through difficult, even hostile territory and terrain.

The Judean hills naturally had valleys. On the side of these valleys goat paths can still be seen. Some of these are particularly steep, dangerous, dark and narrow. Such a terrain has its perils. One false step on these ridges would mean plunging to an instant death in the canyon below. The danger in Bible days was also compounded by the wild beasts which sought to attack the sheep, not to mention the wild men - the robbers and bandits who hid in the surrounding caves, ready to pounce.

When David was a shepherd, he was acquainted with one such notorious valley. So frightening was this valley that it was named accordingly: The *valley of the shadow of death* :-

> The figure . . . of 'the very dark ravine' . . . is that of a dark, rock defile, when the path narrows, the cliffs almost meet towering overhead, and when the trembling sheep, lost upon the mountains, is particularly exposed to the assaults of enemies. Places of this kind occur repeatedly in the gorges

with which the wilderness pastures abound . . .
Huge hyenas, deadly foes to the flock, which hunt
at night in small packs, some going before and some
waiting behind, easily entrap the sheep in these
gloomy gullies. David, therefore, when declaring
his fearlessness, what time he was to go 'through
the very dark ravine', is, by a bold and beautiful
metaphor, expressing his confidence in every time
of danger.

(James Neil, *Everyday Life in Bible Times*, p. 53)

God is with us

*Even though I walk through the valley of the shadow of death,
I fear no evil; for Thou art with me* . . . The verse encapsulates a
Biblical principle, and the principle is this: Safety is not the
absence of danger but the presence of God. *Though I walk in
the midst of trouble, Thou dost preserve my life* (Psalm 138:7).

So the Christian today - just like David then - is
privileged to enjoy the personal presence of God amidst
dangerous circumstances - and who would like to claim that
the world today is any less dangerous than in David's day?
We are surrounded by danger - physical, moral and spiritual
- all of which seek to do us harm and bring us down. The
Bible does not encourage us to bury our heads in the sand. It
would have us beware of the dangers, but it would also have
us be aware of the presence of God with us day by day, in and
through all the dangers we face. Some of the Lord Jesus's last
words to His disciples were these: *I am with you always, to the
close of the age* (Matthew 28:20). *I am with you* (Acts 18:10)
said the risen Lord to Paul, just when he needed such an
assurance. *It is the LORD Who goes before you; He will be with
you, He will not fail you or forsake you* (Deuteronomy 31:8) said
Moses to the people of Israel, as they stood on the brink of the
Promised Land. *The LORD our God is with you wherever you go*

(Joshua 1:9)' said the Lord Himself to Joshua as he took over Moses's responsibility to lead the people.

The God of the Bible therefore is a God Who personally presences Himself with His people in and through this difficult and dangerous world. He will lead us safely home to His house. There we will be eternally saved and eternally safe, for ever out of the reach of both the danger without and the depravity within.

Even though I walk through the valley of the shadow of death, I fear no evil, for Thou art with me, Thy rod and Thy staff they comfort me.

> *Yea, though I walk through death's dark vale*
> *Yet will I fear none ill*
> *For Thou art with me; and Thy rod*
> *And staff me comfort still*

Thou art with me - refers to God's presence in the valley. *Thy rod and Thy staff* refers to God's protection within the valley -*for he who touches you touches the apple of His eye* (Zechariah 2:8). We shall consider this next.

Chapter Seven

THE DIVINE PROTECTION

Thy rod and Thy staff, they comfort me (v.4).

A Shepherd's Equipment

AN EASTERN SHEPHERD WOULD have carried a few 'tools of the trade' with him. Among these would have been a bottle of oil, a small bag or pouch, a sling, a leather bottle of water and a wooden cup, and a rod and a staff. We shall consider these last two items now for they, along with the personal presence of the shepherd, added to the comfort and well-being of the flock. *Thy rod and Thy staff, they comfort me.*

The rod and staff speak of might and mercy respectively. The rod was primarily an offensive weapon, used at close quarters against those who sought to harm the sheep. The staff however was used on the sheep themselves. It resembles the shepherd's crook familiar to those who live in rural areas in the West. Through the careful use of the staff, the shepherd would see that any sheep that were prone to stray were kept safely on the right paths. The rod and the staff then were some of the basic implements of the eastern shepherd. This being said though, they surely point beyond David's immediate time, and tell us of God's almighty protection of His people today.

1. Thy Rod

Defending the Sheep

The rod was a formidable weapon, something like a club. Woe betide any of the sheep's enemies who came into violent contact with the rod! The rod was truly an offensive weapon, and would defeat all the foes of the shepherd and the sheep without mercy.

Interestingly, the image of the rod is taken up in Psalm 2, where it is used to proclaim the certain triumph of the Son of God over all who are opposed to Him. *You shall break them with a rod of iron, and dash them in pieces like a potter's vessel* (Psalm 2:9).

The rod then was only used offensively against the sheep's enemies. Its presence in the shepherd's hand would be a great comfort to the sheep. The rod was not used against the sheep, but it was used for the sheep:-

Counting the Sheep

The Bible also shows how the rod was used by the shepherd as an aid to counting his sheep and thus ensuring that all were 'present and correct.' Here, the shepherd would put his rod horizontally across the entrance to, for example, a sheepfold or a narrow passage way in the valley, block the entrance, and make his flock pass under the rod one at a time.

Whilst they did so, he would count them and also give them a quick 'head to toe' examination, taking any remedial action if it was needed.

In Ezekiel 20:37 God says to His people *I will make you pass under the rod* . . . It shows that God has an intimate knowledge of His people and all that ails them. *The Lord knows those who are His* (2 Timothy 2:19).

Comforting the Sheep

Thy rod . . . comfort(s) me. The fearsome looking rod may not give us the impression of providing comfort, but the sheep would think otherwise! During the darker hours, it was an audible reminder of the shepherd's presence.

Picture the sheep, walking single file through the valley of the shadow of death. Here is a dark and dangerous path if ever there was one. The shepherd is out in front, but what of the sheep at the back? On a twisting path they could lose sight of the shepherd and even fear that he was not there at all. It is here that the rod would give much comfort. The shepherd would bang the rod sharply at the side of the valley. The sound would echo and resonate and reverberate around, and so reassure the sheep of the shepherd's presence. Soon though they would be out of the dark valley. Soon the frightened sheep would meet up again with the shepherd face to face, in the light at the top of the hill.

The application to the Christian is obvious: We can be sure of God's personal presence with us day by day, no matter how dark our circumstances. Our present dark circumstances are not for ever. God will lead us through them, and we will soon meet up with the Shepherd face to face, in the light of the glory land above.

'Thy rod comforts me.' The rod tells us of the sovereign protection of Almighty God over His own.

> *A Sovereign Protector I have*
> *Unseen, yet for ever at hand*
> *Unchangeably faithful to save*
> *Almighty to rule and command*
> *He smiles and my comforts abound*
> *His grace as the dew shall descend*
> *And walls of salvation surround*
> *The soul He delights to defend.*

We notice though that the shepherd also has a staff as well as a rod. Let us consider this implement too:-

2. Thy Staff

Shepherd Thy people with Thy staff, the flock of thine inheritance (Micah 7:14).

The staff corresponds to the western shepherd's crook - such is also sometimes seen in the hand of a 'Bishop' in the liturgical churches, where it symbolises his pastoral care (cure) of souls.

Keeping the Sheep

The staff was used by the shepherd to keep his flock on the paths of righteousness. Should the shepherd notice one of his flock getting out of line, or even veering dangerously near a cliff's edge, he would immediately apply the staff to its hind leg and draw the wayward sheep into alignment with the rest of the flock.

One of the more sordid episodes in David's life shows his being on the receiving end of God's staff himself. II Samuel 11 and 12 relate the sorry story of his adultery with Bathsheba. David had strayed from keeping the commandments of God. God thus, as it were, applied His staff to bring David back into line, employing the prophet Nathan and the sad death of David's child in the process. No one wishes to be on the receiving end of God's staff, yet His shepherd and fatherly love to His children are such that He will not see us going astray. As our God is still the faithful shepherd of His people, we may affirm with 1 Samuel 2:9 *He will guard the feet of His faithful ones.*

Rebuking the Sheep

The shepherd may also use his staff in an even more drastic way on his sheep. A sheep given to rebellion may receive a sharp poke from him, bringing it quickly to order. Such an action may seem cruel to an outsider, yet the shepherd is actually being 'cruel to be kind.' Doing nothing here would be most unkind. Paradoxically, it would actually be cruel and care-less for the shepherd to leave the sheep to its own devices, stray from the flock and then get into danger. God's ways with His children are similar to this. Hebrews 12:6 *For the Lord disciplines him whom He loves, and chastises every son whom He receives.*

Rescuing the Sheep

Finally, we note that the shepherd would also use his staff to rescue the sheep from difficulty. If a sheep had slipped out of human reach, the staff would gently draw it back to the shepherd. If a sheep had got entangled in a thorn bush, the staff could be used to beat away the branches and set the trapped sheep free.

The staff then ensured that the sheep were kept 'on course.' For the staff removed the obstacles from both without and within the sheep, enabling and encouraging it to carry on walking to the pastures of blessing. It is the same in our Christian walk. Our Christian lives can seem so subject to 'fits and starts', but our God will see to it that we go forward. 'Forward still, 'tis Jehovah's will.' *The steps of a man are from the LORD, and He establishes him in whose way He delights; though he fall, he shall not be cast headlong, for the LORD is the stay of his hand* (Psalm 37:24).

So we see how God's rod and staff bring great comfort to His people as they journey heavenward and homeward through this difficult and dangerous earthly wilderness. The Lord Jesus would have us recognise the dangers without and within and pray to our Father in heaven *Lead us not into temptation, but deliver us from evil* (Matthew 6:13), and through the use of our heavenly Shepherd's comforting rod and staff 'suffer not our steps to stray, from the straight and narrow way.' One of the tasks of the shepherd is to protect his sheep from all physical and spiritual harm. *The name of the God of Jacob protect you* (Psalm 20:1).

Chapter Eight

THE DIVINE PREPARATION

*Thou preparest a table before me in the presence of
my enemies* (v.5).

THOSE OF US WHO first heard this Psalm when we were
very young, may have had images of a children's party in our
minds when we first heard this verse - complete with a table
crammed full of sandwiches, cakes, trifles etc. When we grew
older, the image may have been exchanged for that of a
dinner party with our friends. The verse however does not
quite refer to these images! Both images fail to take into
account the original setting of the Psalm in its eastern,
pastoral context.

The Eastern Background

Thou preparest a table before me . . . We have already seen
- in verse 2 - that one of the shepherd's chief tasks is to feed

the flock. *Should not shepherds feed the sheep?* (Ezekiel 34:2). To do this he would have to lead them to suitable pasture land or 'tableland.' On finding such a place, the shepherd would then literally 'prepare a table for them' so that they could eat safely in spite of, or even in the presence of those enemies who sought to do them harm.

How then, would a shepherd prepare a table for his flock? He would do so by scouring the plot of pasture land very carefully. Any stones or rocks which could hurt the sheep as they ate would be raked with his staff and cleared out of harm's way. Also, any nasty looking thistles on the ground would be dug out with his staff and gathered. Perhaps the shepherd would make a fire out of them later. Poisonous plants would be similarly dealt with. Thorn bushes like wise would be hacked down with the rod and staff, lest in its eagerness for food the hungry flock got entangled in them.

On coming to any potholes in the ground, the good shepherd would fill them in, in case they caused his flock to stumble and sprain a leg. Most importantly, the shepherd would be on the look out for any snakes and scorpions such as abound in the Middle East. On finding any, the shepherd would kill them without mercy, striking them on the head with his rod or staff. If he saw a viper's hole, he would pour on hog's oil. The snakes would then be unable to slither up and out and cause their deadly havoc and harm.

All these actions then were included in the act of 'preparing a table' for the flock. They ensured that the vulnerable sheep could pasture in safety 'in the presence of their enemies'. A good shepherd cared for his flock, and the careful preparation of a 'table' for them was part of this care. Looking upward to heaven though, David testified of an infinitely Greater Shepherd. *Thou preparest a table before me in the presence of my enemies.*

The Lord is my strength, at his table I find
The power to defeat all my foes
My life He sustains with His kindness and grace
With blessing my cup overflows.

The Almighty Shepherd and Host

Although the Judean wilderness desert setting of Psalm 23 was barren, and although this world is spiritually barren, God's people yet have a bountiful Shepherd in heaven Who provides for His Own and sees that all their needs are met. The Good Shepherd is also a Host of infinite generosity, infinite in His resources.

In Psalm 78:19, the Israelites asked unbelievingly *Can God spread a table in the wilderness?* The answer of the Bible is a resounding 'YES!' The infinite, all-loving, all-powerful One spreads an abundant table.

The Fabulous Feast of Faith

The Bible uses many ways to describe salvation. It views this greatest of all gifts from many angles. Perhaps one of the simplest ways in which the Bible pictures salvation though, is that of a Divine Feast.

By nature our souls are in peril and starving. Yet God in His goodness and mercy has intervened, and has provided an abundant feast for us, to which He invites us to come, partake, eat and be saved. The theme is common to both Testaments:-

In Isaiah 25:6 God promises through His prophet: *On this mountain the LORD of hosts will make for all peoples a feast of fat things, a feast of wine on the lees, of fat things full of marrow, of wine on the lees well refined* . Then turning to the New Testament, in Matthew 22:1-14 we read of the Lord Jesus telling the 'Parable of the Wedding Feast.' *The kingdom of heaven may be compared to a king who gave a marriage feast for his son, and sent his servants to call those who were invited to the marriage feast* . . . Then in the very last book in the Book, in Revelation 19:9, we read *Blessed are those who are invited to the marriage supper of the Lamb.*

God's people then are characterised by feasting not fasting, plenty not poverty, abundance not abstinence. This is because God has prepared a Feast - a table - for us. God has provided us with Jesus. It is Jesus Who, paradoxically, is both the host and the feast. It is He Who saves and satisfies our hungry souls for time and eternity. *He brought me to the banqueting house, and His banner over me was love* (Song of Solomon 2:4).

The Greatest Feast of All

In the ancient Middle East, a shepherd prepared and provided a table for his flock so they could eat and be saved from starvation. In the spiritual sense, God has similarly provided us with Jesus, so that we may eat and be saved.

The coming of Christ into this world was a carefully prepared coming - prepared by the many Old Testament promises and prophecies, all fulfilled to the letter when the Word became flesh in the virgin's womb. *a body hast Thou prepared for Me* (Hebrews 10:5). The coming of Christ also reveals something of the infinite generosity which abides in the heart of God. In Christ He gave the best He had. *For God so loved the world that He gave His only son, that whoever believes in Him should not perish but have eternal life* (John 3:16).

The True Bread of Heaven

The sheep needed food. A shepherd therefore prepared and provided a table for them. In Christ, Almighty God Himself has provided us with the Bread of Life for our souls.

Jesus is our spiritual sustenance, for Jesus is the Bread of Life. In John 6:35 He said *I am the bread of life; he who comes to Me shall not hunger, and he who believes in Me shall never thirst.* He then went on to explain further *I am the living bread which came down from heaven; if any one eats of this bread he will live for ever, and the bread which I shall give for the life of the world is my flesh* (John 6:51). The verse here takes us to Calvary. In the Bible, all roads lead to Calvary. For Calvary is God's ultimate and final provision for our needy souls. It is through the death of Christ for our sins on Calvary's cross, that we have pardon for sin and peace with God for time and eternity. Trusting in Jesus restores us to fellowship with God. The Bible therefore urges *Believe in the Lord Jesus and you will be saved* (Acts 16:31), or, using the Lord's words and the theme of this chapter 'EAT AND LIVE!' Partake of God's table, for Jesus is the Bread of Life Who alone saves, sustains, satisfies and suffices.

> *Thou art the Bread of Life, O Lord to me*
> *Thy holy Word the truth , that saveth me*
> *Give me to eat and live, with Thee above*
> *Teach me to love the truth, for Thou art love.*

Chapter Nine

THE DIVINE PLENTY

Thou anointest my head with oil, my cup overflows (v.5)

The Eastern Background

Picture the scene. It is evening time in rural Palestine. The sheep are about to retire for the night. They are walking into a sheepfold, going through the entrance one by one, passing under the shepherd's rod. As they pass under the rod, the shepherd's experienced eye is giving each member of the flock a careful examination. He notices that one of them has gashed its head on a boulder . . . Another is limping. It needs to have a thorn removed from its foot. The kindly shepherd drops his rod and halts the flow of sheep. He then proceeds to pour olive oil on the sheep's wounds - oil from the bottle of oil which he always carries with him. *Thou anointest my head with oil.* (It has been suggested that the head here is 'generic' - standing for the sum of the parts).

In Bible times the healing properties of oil were well known. In the parable of the Good Samaritan we read that when the good Samaritan aided the hapless victim, he *bound up his wounds, pouring on oil and wine* (Luke 10:34) - wine as an antiseptic disinfectant, and oil for healing. Similarly in Isaiah 1:6 we read of *bruises and sores and bleeding wounds; . . . pressed out . . . bound up . . . softened with oil.*

PART I : THE PLENTIFUL OIL

Protective Oil

Thou anointest my head with oil . . . In recent years, even in our temperate climate in the West, much has been made of the dangers of over-exposure to the sun and the link between the sun and skin cancer. We are encouraged to use protective sun-tan lotion in the summer.

The sun in the Middle East gets especially fierce. The sun-protecting oil of Psalm 23 is therefore in-line with modern knowledge, even though the Psalm was written some three thousand years ago. Oil on the sheep's head would have protected it from harmful forces . (The oil applied to the head of the sheep may also have acted as an insect repellent, for flying insects attack not the sheep's fleece but its head.)

The Bible reveals that today, the Lord Himself is His people's protection and shield from harmful forces: *The LORD is your keeper; the LORD is your shade on your right hand. The sun shall not smite you by day . . .* (Psalm 121:5,6)

The Holy Spirit of God

In the Bible, oil is often used as a symbol of the Holy Spirit - the Third Person of the blessed Trinity. Prophets, priests and kings of the Old Testament dispensation were all anointed with oil as they embarked upon their respective ministries. It symbolised their being set apart for their special role, and their being divinely equipped for the special tasks they were to undertake. David himself, the human author of our Psalm, may be taken as an example here. 1 Samuel 16:13 relates *Then Samuel took the horn of oil, and anointed him in the midst of his brothers: and the Spirit of the LORD came mightily upon David from that day onwards.*

The Anointed One

The anointing of prophets, priests and kings with oil all pointed forward to the promised Messiah who was to come. The Hebrew word 'messiah' means 'anointed one' - 'Christos' in the Greek, translated into English as 'Christ. ' The Bible clearly reveals that the Lord Jesus is the longed for Messiah, prophesied and pre-figured in the Old Testament Scriptures. *You are the Christ, the Son of the living God* (Matthew 16:16). *God anointed Jesus of Nazareth with the Holy Spirit and with power . . .* (Acts 10:38).

At the inauguration of His public ministry therefore - at His baptism - the Lord Jesus was also especially anointed with the Holy Spirit, following on, furthering and fulfilling the ancient tradition. There at the river Jordan: *the Holy Spirit descended upon Him in bodily form as a dove . . .* (Luke 3:22)

As 'the Anointed One' the Lord Jesus fulfils the three-fold role of prophet, priest and king in His One blessed Person - as the *Shorter Catechism* explains with its characteristically concise Biblical insight:-

> Christ as our Redeemer, executeth the offices of a prophet, of a priest, and of a king . . . (Answer 23).

> Christ executeth the office of a prophet in revealing to us, by His word and Spirit, the will of God for our salvation (Answer 24).

Christ executeth the office of a priest, in His once offering up of Himself a sacrifice to satisfy divine justice, and reconcile us to God; and in making continual intercession for us (Answer 25).

Christ executeth the office of a king, in subduing us to Himself, in ruling and defending us, and in restraining and conquering all His and our enemies (Answer 26).

The Christian's Anointing with Oil

We have already seen how oil was used to aid healing, and that oil is symbolic of the Holy Spirit. Combining both of these, we are reminded of the indispensable role of the Holy Spirit today as God's agent of salvation in the world. It is through the ministry of the Holy Spirit that we receive the ultimate healing - the healing of our broken relationship with God. Whilst it is the death of Christ alone which reconciles us to God, it is through the gracious ministry of the Holy Spirit that we are enabled to make the work of Christ our own and so appropriate all His saving benefits. The Holy Spirit is God's agent of salvation in the world today. It is He Who applies the work of Christ to the human soul and so makes it eternally effective. Without the Spirit's gracious ministry we would never believe in Christ, for the fallen human will is powerless to believe in Jesus in and of itself. We are lost apart from the mighty enabling and assisting of the Holy Spirit. Again, the *Shorter Catechism* clarifies this point most helpfully in the following precise statements which should be carefully considered:-

We are made partakers of the redemption purchased by Christ by the effectual application of it to us by His Holy Spirit (Answer 29).

> The Spirit applies to us the redemption purchased
> by Christ by working faith in us, and thereby unit-
> ing us to Christ in our effectual calling (Answer 30).
>
> Effectual calling is the work of God's Spirit,
> whereby, convincing us of our sin and misery,
> enlightening our minds in the knowledge of Christ
> and renewing our wills, He doth persuade and
> enable us to embrace Jesus Christ, freely offered to
> us in the Gospel (Answer 31).

Thou anointest my head with oil . . . Luke 7:46 shows that having one's head anointed with oil was a sign of honour. The Spirit's anointing of us to eternal salvation is the most incomparable honour of all.

PART II: THE PLENTIFUL WATER

my cup overflows . . .

The shepherd's careful eye might also notice that one of his flock is 'flagging'. One of the flock is thirsty. Perhaps it did not feel the need to partake of the still waters earlier on in the day . It is now suffering the consequences of omitting to drink. No matter. The shepherd had a leather bottle and a wooden cup. Into this wooden cup he would pour a generous portion of water, from which the thirsty sheep would drink gladly. There was nothing mean, stingy or stinting about the shepherd's supply;. . . *my cup overflows.*

The Overflowing Cup

The overflowing cup speaks of abundance. This abundance in turn speaks to the believer again of the abundance of God's munificent salvation. Jesus said of His sheep *I*

came that they might have life and have it abundantly (John 10:10).
We have already seen how water is essential for life, and we
remind ourselves again that the springs of living water which
Christ supplies will never go dry. When we believe in Him
our cup overflows! Jesus still gives the invitation *If any one
thirst let him come to Me and drink. He who believes in Me, as the
Scripture has said, 'Out of his heart shall flow rivers of living
water'* (John 7:38).

The Bitter Cup of Suffering: The Blessed Cup of Salvation

The cup, in Scripture, is symbolic of blessing. In Psalm
16:5 David rejoiced *The LORD is my chosen portion and my cup.*
Psalm 116:12,13 reads *What shall I render to the LORD for all His
bounty to me? I will lift up the cup of salvation and call upon the
name of the LORD.*

It is with great solemnity that we recall that our cup of
salvation is the result of Christ's cup of damnation. On the
cross, Christ drank damnation dry with one dreadful and dire
draught. The anticipation of this cup made Christ shudder
when He prayed in Gethsemene's garden *Father, if Thou art
willing, remove this cup from Me; nevertheless, not my will but
Thine be done* (Luke 22:42).

The will of the Father though was that His Own dear
Son should drink the bitter cup, and we will be eternally thankful that this was so, for His cup of suffering brought us a cup
of eternal salvation. His damnation is our deliverance, His
pain is our pardon and in His cup of dreadful bitterness is our
cup of delightful blessedness. One of the great Christian hymns
puts it like this:-

> *Death and the curse were in our cup*
> *O Christ t'was full for Thee*
> *But Thou has drained the last dark drop*
> *Tis empty now for me*

> *That bitter cup, love drank it up*
> *Now blessing's draught for me.*

Thou anointest my head with oil, my cup overflows. The abundant oil and water here tell us of the divine plenty. Our God is a God of abundant blessing. When we know the Lord as our Shepherd, we have everything we need - and much more besides!

Chapter Ten

THE DIVINE PROMISE

*Surely goodness and mercy shall follow me all the
days of my life . . .* (v.6).

The Good Shepherd's Assistants

WE HAVE ALREADY NOTED that in the Middle East it is a
shepherd's practice to lead his flock from the front, rather than
to drive his flock from behind. Our verse here though reveals
that Almighty God has two 'sheep dogs' following on after
His sheep. The sheep dogs' names are Goodness and Mercy!
Surely goodness and mercy shall follow me all the days of my life.

The verse is both a statement and a promise. It could be
translated *Only goodness and mercy shall follow me all the days of
my life.* The verb employed by the Holy Spirit here reveals
that God's heavenly sheep dogs will not leave us alone. The
verb 'to follow' is a strong one. It literally means 'to pursue.'
God's blessed sheep dogs then are sure to 'hound' us in all
our ways and for all of our earthly days.

> *The Lord has promised good to me*
> *His Word my hope secures*
> *He will my Shield and Portion be*
> *As long as life endures.*

Absolute Certainty

The question is begged: 'How could David be so sure?' The answer is found in David's intimate experience and knowledge of the Shepherd. Having known the Good Shepherd's goodness and mercy in the past and present gave David confidence to trust the self-same Shepherd in the future. Whilst David might fail the Shepherd, he was adamant that the Shepherd would never fail him.

David and His Bible

David's certainty may also be explained in the light of the Scriptures that he had. Although David lacked the privilege of possessing the complete Bible which we have, in David's day, the Torah - the five books of Moses - had already been written by the inspiration of the Holy Spirit. David's certainty then was grounded in the revelation of God given to him in the Bible of his day. David would have known the verse in Exodus 34:6: *The LORD, the LORD, a God merciful and gracious, slow to anger, and abounding in steadfast love and faithfulness* . . . David believed God's Word. Knowing the verse, he acted upon it, and found in it an anchor for his soul. We may do the same and more so, for we have a complete Bible. David lived BC, but we live AD. In Christ - 'Great David's Greater Son' - we have more knowledge of God than David ever had. *We have the prophetic word made more sure* (2 Peter 1:19). *No one has ever seen God; the only Son, Who is in the bosom of the Father, He has made Him known* (John 1:18).

Goodness and Mercy

Surely goodness and mercy shall follow me all the days of my life. Here then are God's attendants - attendants who follow us for all of our days. In His goodness, God showers upon us blessing upon blessing, more than we can ask or think, and more than we ever deserve. In His mercy though God refrains from giving us what we really deserve. Apart from God's goodness and mercy we would certainly be doomed in time and damned for eternity. Let us now look a little more closely at these 'heavenly sheep dogs.' Goodness and mercy are 'divine attributes' - characteristic qualities of the God of the Bible:-

1. Goodness

Berkhof defines God's goodness as 'that perfection of God which prompts Him to deal bountifully and kindly with all His creatures' (*Systematic Theology* p.70). If we open the Bible anywhere, we will see the goodness of God somewhere. *Thou art good and doest good . . .* (Psalm 119:68). *O how abundant is Thy goodness, which Thou hast laid up for those who fear Thee, and wrought for those who take refuge in Thee, in the sight of the sons of men* (Psalm 31:19).

Then when we consider our personal experience, we have to confess that every breath we take and every meal we eat has its source in the goodness of God. We are dependent upon Him for all things. His goodness caused our existence in the first place, and His goodness has sustained us to the present hour. *In Him we live and move and have our being* (Acts 17:28). *He did good and gave you from heaven rains and fruitful seasons, satisfying your hearts with food and gladness* (Acts 14:17).

The Good and the Best

The Christian however will go further here, for a Christian confesses to being a special and specific recipient of God's goodness. A Christian has experienced the goodness of God in a way that infinitely 'out-blesses' all the good things of this life, for whilst God gives life to all, He only bestows eternal life on the Christian believer. Salvation is a result of God's special, specific and sovereign saving grace and goodness in Jesus Christ. *When the goodness and loving kindness of God our Saviour appeared, He saved us . . .* (Titus 3:4,5). In Jesus the goodness of God reached its culmination and climax. Jesus is God's *inexpressible gift* (2 Corinthians 9:15). *He . . . did not spare His own Son but gave Him up for us all . . .* (Romans 8:32).

The goodness of God then has created us, sustained us and also saved us. We, like David, have just cause to be confident that such a goodness will not leave us alone.

Only Goodness

The Apostle Paul had a similar confidence in God's goodness. Paul was confident that the goodness of God extends to both the major and minor details of our lives. Paul would even propound that 'ill that He blesses is our good.' In Romans 8:28 Paul wrote *We know that in everything God works for good with those who love Him, who are called according to His purpose.* This takes us into the realms of God's providence. The *Shorter Catechism* defines God's providence as 'His most holy, wise and powerful preserving and governing all His creatures and all their actions.'

Knowing that God is working literally everything out for our greater blessing is a supreme comfort for the Christian - especially during a time of trial. Whilst dark providences may make the non-Christian despair, the Christian will seek to walk by faith, and seek to see the good, wise and all-loving hand of God in the unwelcome circumstances which come our way. *We know that in everything God works for good with those who love Him . . .* In our darker times, we have a refuge. *The LORD is good, a stronghold in the day of trouble; He knows those who take refuge in Him* (Nahum 1:7).

The first sheep dog hounding our steps then is God's goodness. *O give thanks to the LORD for He is good, for His steadfast love endures for ever* (Psalm 136:1).

> *How good is the God we adore*
> *Our faithful unchangeable Friend*
> *His love is as great as His power*
> *And knows neither measure nor end!*

Goodness however has a companion; its name is Mercy:-

2. Mercy

Mercy, says Louis Berkhof 'may be defined as the goodness or love of God shown to those who are in misery or distress, irrespective of their deserts' (*Systematic Theology* p. 72).

The Christian's theme-song is surely 'A debtor to mercy alone.' In His mercy God spared us the judgment we deserve for our sin. In mercy He spared us, even though He did not spare His own dear Son. In His mercy, God sent His own dear Son as our Saviour-substitute to pay and suffer the punishment which we deserve for our sin. *Sending His own Son in the likeness of sinful flesh and for sin, He condemned sin in the flesh* (Romans 8:3). *He . . . did not spare His own Son but gave Him up for us all* (Romans 8:32). Our salvation then is sourced in God's mercy - His pardoning mercy in the crucified Christ. If we are believers we can testify that God's mercy has followed us and found us. He has *saved us, not because of deeds done by us in righteousness, but in virtue of His own mercy* (Titus 3:5). In Christ, God's mercy became incarnate.

Chesed

The word translated mercy in Psalm 23:6 is the Hebrew word 'Chesed.' Chesed is a key word of the Old Testament. It is actually somewhat difficult to translate, but terms such as 'steadfast love, mercy, grace, covenant loyalty, loving kindness, faithfulness, unfailing love' are aimed in the right direction. Chesed is inextricably bound up with the covenant which God makes with His people. As the Covenant is a key which unlocks the whole Bible, we mention it here:-

The Covenant of Grace

The Covenant is God's bond - the binding bond which He makes with His people. In God's sovereign covenant of grace, He sovereignly chooses for Himself a people and pledges Himself to them with the promise *I will be their God, and they shall be my people* (Hebrews 8:10). This covenant results in fellowship with God for time and eternity.

In Jesus, the covenant reached its fulfilment. His death on the cross inaugurated a new covenant. His death on the cross dealt with those sins which impede a sinner from having fellowship with a holy God. At the Lord's Supper, Jesus spoke of His impending death in these terms: *this is my blood of the new covenant which is poured out for many for the forgiveness of sins* (Matthew 26:28).

A Christian then, is in covenant with God, for God has entered into an unbreakable covenant with us. A Christian can sing 'I am His and He is mine, for ever and for ever.' This being so, how can we ever be doubtful of God's blessed favour in this life and the next? *Surely goodness and mercy shall follow me all the days of my life.* We have a divine hope and a divine help because we are pursued by two divine hounds! We are also assured of a divine home, and to this we will turn in our final chapter.

Goodness and mercy all my days
shall surely follow me
And in God's house for evermore
My dwelling place shall be.

Chapter Eleven

THE DIVINE PROSPECT

And I shall dwell in the house of the LORD for ever (v.6).

WITH THE ASSURANCE OF this exquisite prospect - the prospect of enjoying fellowship with God for ever - David puts down his pen and concludes this pearl of Psalms. David was convinced that the fellowship he enjoyed with God now would continue - in fact it would get even better - for all eternity. In knowing the eternal God as His Shepherd, David was assured of a happy life, a happy death and a happy eternity. As a consequence of knowing the eternal God as his Shepherd, David lacked nothing and would lack nothing. All God's people may testify the same, and all God's people will testify the same. 'One day we shall see that nothing - literally nothing - which could have increased our eternal happiness has been denied us, and that nothing - literally nothing - that could have reduced that happiness has been left with us' (James Packer, *Knowing God* p.308).

And so through all the length of days
Thy goodness faileth never
Good Shepherd may I sing Thy praise
Within Thy house for ever.

The Eastern Background

The sheep alluded to in Psalm 23 are a flock destined for life not death. In Bible times some sheep were reared for death - to be slain in sacrifice - and other sheep were reared for their wool. Psalm 23 has these latter in mind. The sheep behind Psalm 23 were expected to live out their full life-span.

Rev Philip Meader in his talk on 'The Eastern Shepherd' mentions a very touching custom concerning the shepherd and his sheep. He tells how an old sheep - one whose limbs no longer fitted it for wandering from pasture to pasture - would not be slaughtered once its best days were gone. No. An old sheep, unfit for wandering would actually be taken into the shepherd's own home! The shepherd was now emotionally tied to the sheep. The shepherd was just unable to cast out his sheep after so many years of close companion-ship. The old sheep would therefore spend the twilight of its life in the shepherd's own home - it would take its place as an honoured family pet.

Eternal Security

The above custom reminds us of our Good Shepherd's way with His sheep. Jesus assures all who believe in Him *He who comes to Me I will not cast out* (John 6:37). The Bible teaches the eternal security of the soul united to Jesus in saving faith. Jesus will never disown His own sheep. He saves and He keeps for ever. In John 10:27,28 Jesus gives the reassurance *My sheep hear My voice , and I know them, and they follow Me; and I give them eternal life and they shall never perish, and no one shall snatch them out of my hand.*

> *Loving Shepherd of Thy sheep*
> *Keep Thy lambs in safety keep*
> *Nothing can Thy power withstand*
> *None can pluck them from Thy hand.*

Our Shepherd's House

I shall dwell in the house of the LORD for ever.

David only had five books of the Bible, whereas we are blessed with sixty six. Yet inspired by the same Holy Spirit Who in time was to complete the whole Volume, it comes as no surprise to see that David's sentiments are identical to those of Paul when he wrote a millennium and a half later than David's time. The Holy Spirit inspired Paul to write *for we know that if the earthly tent we live in is destroyed, we have a building from God, a house not made with hands, eternal in the heavens* (2 Corinthians 5:1). Paul too was adamant that one day *we shall always be with the Lord* (1 Thessalonians 4:17).

For the Christian, the best is yet to be. We are saved by grace, but destined for glory. *Thou dost guide me with Thy counsel, and afterward Thou wilt receive me to glory* (Psalm 73:24). *The LORD is my shepherd . . . He leads me in paths of righteousness . . . I shall dwell in the house of the LORD for ever* (vv. 1,3,6).

My Father's House

Those prone to speculating about heaven need speculate no longer but turn to the Bible. The Bible, albeit somewhat rarely, actually lifts the veil and gives us a peek into the life which is to come - the blessedness which awaits the Christian! We may be sure though that the actual reality will be better, greater, richer and fuller than we can ever conceive or comprehend in this life, handicapped by sin as we are. According to the Lord Jesus though, heaven is home. Heaven is a prepared home for a prepared people. In John 14:2,3 Jesus stated *In my Father's house are many rooms; if it were not so, would I have told you that I go to prepare a place for you? And when I go and prepare a place for you, I will come again and will take you to myself, that where I am you may be also.*

> *O think of the home over there*
> *By the side of the river of light*
> *Where the saints all immortal and fair*
> *Are robed in their garments of white.*

There is no place like home. After a day away at work, or even after a happy holiday in a luxurious hotel, it is always good to come home and be at ease amidst our own comfortable and familiar surroundings in the company of those we love.

'Home is where the heart is', and every Christian has a 'homing instinct' for heaven, the glorious house of our heavenly Father. Heaven is our eternal home! There we will not only be eternally saved but also eternally safe, secure and happy. In heaven we will know unblemished and unhindered fellowship with our God for ever - that fellowship for which we were designed and that fellowship for which we long but never seem to attain here on earth. In glory though, we will be 'made perfectly blessed in the full enjoying of God to all eternity' (*Shorter Catechism*). In glory, we will continue no less to enjoy the blessed friendship and fellowship begun here on earth with the Good Shepherd - the Good Shepherd Who laid down His life for the sheep. *For the Lamb in the midst of the throne will be their shepherd, and He will guide them to springs of living water; and God will wipe away every tear from their eyes* (Revelation 7:17).

Conclusion

Many of the one hundred and fifty Psalms which comprise the Psalter are either prayers or expressions of deep longing and aspiration. Psalm 23 though is none of these. Psalm 23 is simply a statement of fact. Psalm 23 is an open and honest testimony to David's own personal experience. Sinner though he was, David could yet confess *The LORD is my shepherd, I shall not want* . It is a testimony to the grace of God and the God of grace.

Although Psalm 23 was written by David, the Psalm just cannot be confined to David's time, just as it cannot be confined to its middle eastern pastoral setting. The God testified to in Psalm 23 has not changed. *I the LORD do not change* (Malachi 3:6). The Shepherd of Israel is our eternal contemporary. When we know Christ as our all sufficient Saviour, even we may utter the heart-felt confession: *The LORD is my shepherd.* And knowing the Lord as our Shepherd, He will surely meet our every need both here and hereafter.

Now may the God of peace Who brought again from the dead our Lord Jesus, the great shepherd of the sheep, by the blood of the eternal covenant, equip you with everything good that you may do His will, working in you that which is pleasing in His sight, through Jesus Christ; to Whom be glory for ever and ever. Amen (Hebrews 13:20,21).

SOLI DEO GLORIA

EPILOGUE

The Lord's my Shepherd, I'll not want:
He makes me down to lie
In pastures green; He leadeth me
The quiet waters by.

My soul He doth restore again;
And me to walk doth make
Within the paths of righteousness,
E'en for His own Name's sake.

Yea, though I walk in death's dark vale,
Yet will I fear none ill;
For Thou art with me; and Thy rod
And staff me comfort still.

My table Thou hast furnished
In presence of my foes;
My head Thou dost with oil anoint,
And my cup overflows.

Goodness and mercy all my life
Shall surely follow me;
And in God's house for evermore
My dwelling place shall be.

Psalm 23 (Metrical Version)
The Scottish Psalter, 1650

BIBLIOGRAPHY

The Hebrew Bible ('Tanach') (edited by Norman H. Snaith, British and Foreign Bible Society)

The Holy Bible (Revised Standard Version)

Learn Biblical Hebrew (John H. Dobson, Summer Institute of Linguistics)

New Bible Dictionary (Second Edition, Ed., Inter Varsity Press)

New Bible Commentary Revised (Ed., Inter Varsity Press)

Exploring The Psalms, Volume I (John Phillips, Loizeaux Brothers)

The Treasury of David (C. H. Spurgeon, Marshall, Morgan and Scott)

He Leadeth Me (C. W. Slemming, Christian Literature Crusade)

The Pearl of Psalms (George Henderson, B. McCall Barbour)

Everyday Life in Bible Times (James Neil, Olive Tree Press)

Handbook of Life in Bible Times (J. A. Thompson, Inter Varsity Press)

The New Manners and Customs of Bible Times (Ralph Gower, Moody Press)

Knowing God (James I. Packer, Hodder and Stoughton)

My Father's House (Timothy Cross, Ambassador)

The Westminster Shorter Catechism

Systematic Theology (Louis Berkhof, Banner of Truth)

By the same author

WALKING WITH JESUS

BY Timothy Cross

Walk where Christ walked, starting with His birth
and ending with His ascension into heaven. *Walking
with Jesus* describes and considers ten milestones in
the life of Jesus. The ten unforgettable chapters of
this book were described by one reviewer as "a
devotional classic."

COMFORT FROM THE BIBLE

BY Timothy Cross

In this book Dr. Cross illustrates how to draw comfort from the Scripture in your darkest days. The
references he uses are just what you need for any trial
you may encounter. God's Word is the only source
we need to lift the veil of depression, the weight of
sorrow, or the load of responsibility.

SCENT FROM HEAVEN

BY Timothy Cross

Can any fragrance be as sweet as the loveliness of
Christ? In this rich, devotional, typological study, the
author points out that our blessing derives from
Christ's bruising. As fragrant plants do not yield
their sweet perfume unless they are crushed, like-
wise, if our Saviour had not been crushed at Calvary,
He could not have given His sweetest pardon.

MY FATHER'S HOUSE

BY Timothy Cross

The glory that awaits the child of God is unspeakable and unimaginable. Beautifully pictured in this book is a small glimpse of what heaven holds for us. After a peek into heaven, you will view your day-to-day tasks in a different light.

A STRING OF PEARLS
Treasures from the Bible

BY Timothy Cross

In this simple but profound book, the author has mined some of the precious treasures of the Bible for you. Containing a wealth of interest, intrigue and inspiration, an enjoyable, enlightening, edifying and enriching reading experience awaits you.

A POSTCARD FROM PAUL
The letter of Paul to Philemon

BY Timothy Cross

Paul's short letter to Philemon is one of the neglected legacies of the Holy Spirit to the Christian Church - but it is a mine of blessing. *A Postcard From Paul* brings this largely unknown letter alive for you today with an agreeable blend of clear explanation, contemporary application and Christ-centred devotion.